Reimagine YOUR BRAND

HOW TO CREATE IMPACT FOR YOUR BUSINESS

Reimagine
YOUR BRAND

HOW TO CREATE IMPACT FOR YOUR BUSINESS

DONNA GALASSI

BLUE ▽ ZENITH

Reimagine Your Brand: How to Create Impact for Your Business
Published by Blue Zenith LLC
Centennial, Colorado

Library of Congress Control Number: 2018906331
GALASSI, DONNA, Author
REIMAGINE YOUR BRAND
DONNA GALASSI

ISBN: 978-0-692-12542-7

BUSINESS & ECONOMICS / Entrepreneurship
BUSINESS & ECONOMICS / Women in Business

QUANTITY PURCHASES: Schools, companies, professional groups,
clubs, and other organizations may qualify for special terms when
ordering quantities of this title. For information, email Books@
BlueZenith.com.

For Shayden Colvin.
You lived life with wonder:
boldly, authentically, and with heart.

Contents

introduction

Branding You and Your Business

As an entrepreneur running a service-based business, you know that competition is fierce. You strive to stand out as unique, attract the right clients, and grow your reputation in your industry. You look for methods to get results that drive your bottom line. The essential elements of success are to rise above the competition and grab the attention of potential clients.

In today's busy marketplace, the noise of marketing and endless options surrounds clients. There is always something demanding their attention—away from you. It's becoming more difficult to be heard through that noise and connect with clients.

You may think of branding as your logo and colors, but it is much more than that. Perhaps you have thought of branding as something that only big companies need, but all business-es need branding. Entrepreneurs and small businesses need a solid brand to highlight their uniqueness and innovation of their offerings. The outcome of good branding is obvious. It attracts the right clients, sells what you do, and keeps your business dreams growing.

What is a brand anyway? Branding means different things to different people. Your logo, colors, and fonts are pieces of your branding, but your brand goes far deeper. Is it also your offerings? Definitely. What you offer and how you market it is a big part of your brand. Marketing to your strengths and uniqueness will help establish your business as distinct and different.

Is branding also how you treat your customers? Yes, ab-solutely! The way you treat your customers and what they say about working with you is the most critical piece of your brand.

With so many varying elements, what are the most impor-tant factors that define your brand? They include establishing what your brand stands for and what your customers think and say about you. In other words, your customers take the image you create and convey a message of your brand to the public. Knowing this can help you mold your brand over time into something that targets and grabs the attention of customers.

In this book, I'm going to talk about two perspectives. You and your customers'. You'll hear me say that you are the one unique element in your business. I'll also say that your brand is designed and created from your customers' perspective.

So how do these two perspectives come together? A brand becomes a powerful tool when your clients see themselves in your message and connect with you and your vision. In other words, the magic of branding happens at the place where you and your clients cross paths and click. This book and the exercises in the following chapters will guide you on a branding journey to pinpoint that magical intersection.

This book is a culmination of my journey of starting a business and redefining my brand. There are countless books about branding out there, so what makes this one different? I'm an entrepreneur, and I serve entrepreneurs. I know what's important to us. For us, business is personal. Our clients are people that we know personally, and we build relationships and share a journey with them over time.

I developed this branding guide for heart-centered, purpose-driven entrepreneurs who are driven by the desire to make an impact in the world. It is for entrepreneurs who want to make a difference in the lives of the people they work with. If that describes you, read on. This book will expand your idea of what a brand is, and what you need to do to stand out unique and distinct from your competition. It will also help you gain the insight needed to create intention and strategy in building your brand—the most essential tool in building success.

The book will guide you through each area of brand building. Through stories, exercises, and introspection, you will dive deeply into understanding your business, your competitors, and the pool of potential customers. You will gain the knowledge and tools needed to build a compelling brand that captures your unique business culture and how it addresses your clients' needs.

As you work through this book, you'll learn how to position your business for growth by discovering the importance of yourself in your brand foundation. You will also travel through a personal journey that will help you discover and tell your story and incorporate it into your brand. Each exercise in this book is designed to capture a part of your past, present, and future as that relates to your business and life. While taking this step into self-discovery, you will be challenged to walk in your client's shoes to discover insights into your ideal clients and identify a better experience for their journeys.

You will become the mapmaker who charts the map and route of where you want your business to be and how to get it there. Ultimately, you'll pinpoint the magical crossroads where your story meets your customers' struggles, and they connect with you.

MAKE AN IMPACT

I believe that everything needs to start with your clients. From your offerings to the delivery of them, it's all about making an impact on your clients' lives. Your brand and your digital presence should be a resource that attracts the right clients and works as hard as you do in supporting that goal.

I've been in the technology industry my entire working career, from working for large corporations to small lean, start-up businesses. In 2009, I founded my marketing business, Blue Zenith. The mantra of my business is: Human Centered. Customer Centric. Experience Focused.

To me, it sums up everything we do, from how we create the experience to how we deliver it. The experience is the heart of my business and the driving force behind every brand we help clients develop.

It's my mission to provide service-based businesses and entrepreneurs with solutions to better connect with clients using the tools at hand and the trends in marketing. A critical aspect of that is leveraging social media. Social media came storming into pop culture and attracted the masses in the fall of 2006 when Facebook opened to the public and invited everyone onto its platform. It forever changed how we communicate online, including how we connect with our clients from our business websites.

Without an understanding of social media, digital trends, and online tools, your business can appear less than it is, or worse, it can look like every other business. You risk being perceived as a commodity—something that anyone can do. Your business becomes a widget replaceable by the next competitor who is cheaper and faster. It devalues your worth.

I want to change that. You are worthy of so much more. I want to help you make the biggest impact you can in the lives of your ideal clients. It is my mission in this book to help you give voice to your message.

FOCUS ON THE EXPERIENCE

Your brand should communicate who you are and why you are different in a story. This story tells the world how you treat your clients, how you market your offerings, and how your business is unique and distinct.

Your brand is also how your business is perceived in the marketplace by your customers and the public. Ultimately, your brand is defined by how your clients feel after working with you. The experience you deliver is everything. It should inspire your clients and provide hope, confidence, fulfillment, joy—whatever it is that you deliver through your offerings.

To accomplish this, you must incorporate everything you've ever thought of as a brand and build an experience around what your clients need and expect from you. There are endless other options from which customers can choose for the services you offer. To capture their attention, you need to create an ideal client experience every way you can through everything you do.

Consider Amazon. Consumers had first thought of Amazon as a company that sells things, but the perception has evolved. Now Amazon is often considered a company that helps people find and buy things they need in the fastest, most convenient way possible. Amazon helps today's busy consumers save time and effort. That shift in thinking from merely selling to providing an experience was instrumental in creating Amazon's brand.

With that concept in mind, I want you to begin to shift your thinking to ways you can help your potential clients solve their challenges and provide a positive, memorable experience they can't get anywhere else.

Imagine your brand is all these things:

- A true representation of your values and culture that are foundational to your business

- A resource for clients when they seek information
- A cache of answers to questions your potential clients have during their decision-making process
- A showcase where people go to learn about what you do, why it's important to you, and the difference you make in their lives
- A platform where you, a leader in your industry, share your philosophy and nuggets of information that your clients need to be successful
- A way to present the promise that you ultimately deliver
- A means for your clients to learn about you and choose to do business with you

I challenge you to not swim in the sea of sameness. So many entrepreneurs can't communicate why they are different, or they are afraid of being too bold and taking a different approach than their competitors. Many of you know you need to be distinct but don't know what that means or how to get started. This book holds some of the answers. The rest lies in you and your ability to work through these exercises.

chapter one

The Three Non-Negotiables of Success

Life has a way of finding you. Sometimes people make their own success, and sometimes they're pulled towards their destiny. In the second case, it's fate that leads them to something great. And so, it was with me.

I am an entrepreneur. I have always known that one day I was going to be my own boss, running my own business. Both my parents ran their own business, and it seemed natural for me to do the same. But, as always, life got in the way. I went to college, got married, had two children, and moved away from Florida, where I had gone to high school and college.

My first job out of college was at Honeywell in Clearwater, Florida, working as a software engineer. I was looking for a new adventure and was excited when Honeywell transferred me to their Littleton division, bringing my husband and me to Colorado. After working as a software developer and engineer for more than eleven years in everything from small businesses to large corporations, I found myself at a juncture.

In the summer of 2007, a perfect storm blew apart my life. Three pivotal events happened that changed my path and led me to start my own business. The first, and most important thing was that my daughter, my oldest child, had graduated from high school and was on her way to college. My family and my role as a mother was about to change drastically.

That summer, I was working at a small local business as a software engineer in the technology department. The business provided reports to real estate investors and the investors used the reports to analyze undervalued properties before purchasing them for their real estate portfolios. The company employed about a dozen people, and I was part of the technology team that produced those reports.

One day, I went into the office to pick up my paycheck. To my surprise, there were no paychecks for the technology department. Our team was excluded in the salary funding for that pay period. The five of us in that department were given an excuse about a funding issue and asked to come back the next day. Day after day, I asked for my paycheck and received another excuse for why it was not there.

After more than two weeks, I came to a major crossroads. I had no faith that I would ever be paid for my time. At the same time, I was still working and racking up unpaid paychecks, which I had no hope of seeing. I remember the day I made the pivotal decision. After hearing yet another excuse, I sat at my desk and thought about my family and what my teenagers had planned for their day. At that moment, I realized that my time was more valuable to my family and me. My skills and expertise demanded respect. Something clicked. I simply stood up and left.

I could say I was laid off because that is something that everyone understands. The truth is quite different; I stopped getting paid, so I stopped going. Simple as that.

That was the first step I took into my own power.

What I didn't realize at that moment was that I had given myself a gift—the gift of time. I found that I had more time to see my daughter. Anyone who has teenagers knows how little parents may see of them before they go off to college. They are often out with friends, on their way to see their friends, or coming home from seeing friends. You feel like you never have time to connect. Once I was no longer working, I was more accessible and could connect with her in a meaningful way between her social engagements.

When I look back at the summer of 2007, my strongest memories are not of watching the economy slide into recession or of losing half our family income at a time when it was most needed. I remember the day we packed a picnic lunch and my kids, and I hiked St Mary's Glacier in the Rocky Mountains of Colorado. I think of another day when we piled into the car and drove to Estes Park and Rocky Mountain National Park. I cherish the times we were able to be a family for a brief, priceless moment in time.

Once my daughter went off to college, I realized that it was not a good time to look for a job—nor was it a good time to start my own business. Yet, that was exactly what I decided to do. I had always known I was destined to be an entrepreneur, but the time never seemed right. You know what I mean—how we all wait for the perfect time to take our first step towards our dreams. The trouble is, there's never a perfect time. I had been kicked into this situation and realized that although the time wasn't right, it really was. I put myself first and trusted myself and my skills in forging my new normal.

And so, I took the road to starting my own business, Blue Zenith. I began operating as a sole proprietor in 2008 and filed my LLC in early 2009. Blue Zenith started as a web design business. Through time, I came to realize that entrepreneurs needed more than just a website to be effective and compete. They needed websites that brought their hearts and souls into their visuals and message.

Through my journey of self-discovery, Blue Zenith grew to become a business that delivers websites that serve as a digital marketing storefront. The websites we design greet a business's customers with the same personality they would meet if they walked in the door of a brick-and-mortar store.

GETTING OUTSIDE THE COMFORT ZONE

When I started my journey as an entrepreneur, I was an introvert. I had never networked in my life or put myself on the line because I hadn't needed to step far outside my comfort zone. I soon realized that if I wanted to succeed, I had to push myself further into uncomfortable situations for an introvert—and that meant meeting people and networking.

I joined the local chamber of commerce, taking baby steps at first. I would time myself at their big networking events. At first, it was a challenge to stay for fifteen minutes and meet two people. By the end of a few months, I was closing out the networking event because I had gotten to know so many people. What a passage that was for me. Soon, I was joining other networking and leads group to meet as many people as possible. As I added confidence and contacts, I grew my business.

It wasn't easy. Starting my own business during the worst of the 2008 recession was a struggle, and each client and every dollar I made was a celebration. Though getting business was hard, making business connections wasn't. Most of the Chamber of Commerce business owners were active in many chamber events, so there was a time and a place to get to know the business community.

That worked to my advantage. I learned that by building connections and relationships within the community, I fueled the customer base of my business. I now have built a family-run business that supports my employee son, another full-time employee, and my mom, who works as a part-time assistant. Through strategically working on each challenge presented to me, I was able to create the family-run business that I'd always wanted.

STAND IN YOUR POWER

Being an entrepreneur has made me stand in my own power. Starting your own business is as raw and real as it gets. It takes guts to know that your actions directly impact whether you get to continue your business for another day. It's scary, exciting, and fulfilling. What fuels me each morning is the fact that I get to help other entrepreneurs fulfill his or her purposes by helping them impact their client's lives. It's quite a powerful thing.

My personal story is deeply intertwined with my business. I can't talk about one without the other. It's a story of making my own path through life and taking my strengths and making them into a successful, thriving business. From what I have learned on this journey, I can help you, my fellow entrepreneurial warriors. Your ability to be successful is directly related to how bold you stand in your power and how confident you are in your talents and gifts. That, my friends, is the heart and soul of creating a brand.

In this workbook, you'll find pieces of my story, stories of clients that have come before you, and the tools you'll need to find your path to building a successful brand. The exercises will guide you to create a brand that matches your heartfelt purpose and communicates your story. You'll step confidently into your strengths and learn more about your ideal clients, why they need you, and how you can better connect with their journey. I challenge you to be bold, to be big, and to get ready to create the brand that is waiting inside you.

DO YOU HAVE WHAT IT TAKES?

My journey into business taught me the three key non-negotiables of success. I learned I needed to step into them and completely commit to becoming the person that deserved to triumph.

Branding boldly requires guts and these three non-negotiables of success:

1. **Believe in yourself.** There are so many things working against us. Don't be one of them! You must believe in yourself and your dream so strongly that you see yourself as a brand, as something worthy of being called a business. Your belief must be stronger than the naysayers. It must be more significant than the challenging circumstances in your life. To have a fighting chance, your dream must be something that you want more than anything else. If you believe in yourself, you have what it takes. You know what you need, and you do it. You see opportunity when others may not. You need to see that as your destiny and purpose.

2. **Value your talents and gifts and knowledge.** Know you are worthy of respect. You and your expertise are gifts that should be treasured. You cannot build a business if you don't value what you bring to it. If you don't appreciate your talents, then how do you expect your customers to appreciate you? How can you demand respect if you don't respect yourself first? Be confident that you and your skills and expertise are enough.

3. **Be willing to do the hard work.** This is the most important one. Without this one, you can't make your dream happen. Being successful is not easy. Each day there will be a new struggle, a new challenge to face, and a

new lesson to learn. Face each day with a promise to yourself that you are moving forward with no option to fail. Remember that nothing in life worth fighting for has ever been easy.

In my journey, I now see that if I hadn't valued my skills and time, I wouldn't have left my job. If I hadn't believed in my ability to succeed, I wouldn't have started my business. And if I hadn't been willing to step bravely into fear, I would never have grown my business to where it is now. These three things define my transformation and guide my process.

It takes buckets of confidence to wrap the three non-negotiables of success into your life. It's not easy to build that kind of self-assurance, but you can start by remembering that every one of us brings special talents and a spark of uniqueness to this world.

But it goes deeper than that. These three non-negotiable traits fuel our inner power, our *superpower.* If you have the three non-negotiable traits, I know you've got what it takes. You have the power, the superpower.

Now, let's explore what you need to define your brand.

chapter two

Bringing YOU into Your Brand

Let's get real.

Why is brand building so important? Because there are more than one billion websites around the world and count-less pages of Google results when you search online for your service. The competition seems endless, and that is the big-gest challenge we face in business.

Most entrepreneurs don't have endless piles of money to throw at marketing. Our strategies must be streamlined and focused on our clients. We must define our purpose and craft a message that connects to the type of clients we want to attract. By narrowing our focus to these clients, we can tailor our message to bond in a meaningful way.

Let's back up a step. What should you be aiming for? I want you to envision your business as a referral-based business, one based on customer loyalty—or brand loyalty, as I like to think of it. This means that you attract the right customers, the ones who come back to you again and again. They shout your praises and bring new customers into the fold. Isn't that what you want to build?

But with all that competition out there, how do you stand out? It seems an impossible task, but assessing the competition will reveal how you are distinct. Reviewing your competitors will show you that no one else can be you. You are the one thing that is unique and different about your business.

Capturing and showcasing your personality, voice, and expertise are keys to standing out among the pages of Google results. Because you already have what you need to be distinct, you now need the courage to stand in your own power and broadcast that. Remember those three non-negotiables of success?

- You believe in yourself.
- You value your talents, gifts, and knowledge.
- You are willing to do the hard work.

Here they come back with full force. Embrace what makes you, you. Embrace your strengths and your weaknesses. Build your business based on your talents, gifts, and knowledge, and hire skilled people to support you in areas that are outside your expertise.

It's also essential to define your brand by your strengths and your moral compass—your values and beliefs. Another key element of a strong brand is communicating the story of how you got started in business. Clients will connect with your personal story, and once connected with you, clients will be more likely to return to you. In other words, your personal story will help build a business based on brand loyalty.

THE STUMBLING BLOCKS

Branding can be a powerful tool—if developed correctly. The problem is that not enough small businesses and entrepreneurs do it effectively. They may not be consistent with their brand across all media. Their message or their voice may change, creating a patchy or unpredictable experience. Their brand may also not reflect the needs of their clients or show their clients how they will solve their struggles or problems.

The purpose of a brand is to attract the right clients who grow your business. Building a strong brand will expand the reach of your business beyond your circle of friends and influence. It should shorten the time it takes someone to get to know you, like you, and trust you. It should also help clients see what you can do for them and then buy from you.

Remember, you can't be everything to everyone. To grow your business through branding, you must identify your niche and the people you best serve. That isn't everyone. The sooner you come to understand that, the sooner we can work to create the brand that is uniquely you.

Insight into YOU Exercise

Creating a brand starts with your personality, your vision of success, and your moral compass, which includes beliefs and values. I will start your branding journey by asking a few deceptively simple questions. We begin by looking into you before diving into your business. Your answers here will help you complete later exercises and worksheets within this workbook.

Your core beliefs are the way you see the world and your role in it. What are your core beliefs that guide you through decisions each day?

_____

_____

_____

Your business takes on a lot of your personality traits. Let's identify some of your main personality traits and how the world perceives you. What personality traits best describe you?

_____

_____

_____

Let's envision our best life and the role we play in that life. That is our vision of success. What does that look like to you? What is your version of success?

_____

_____

_____

What are the moral compass values that guide you through life? Examples include kindness matters, respect always, embrace differences, and family first.

_____

_____

_____

Your personality, your vision of success, and your moral compass—what do these have to do with building a brand? Well, to me, they are everything. Let these answers be a reference as you go through the remaining exercises as we delve deeper into developing your brand.

Insight into Your Business Exercise

Now let's begin thinking in terms of your business.

What core beliefs are foundational for your business? These can be different than your personal core beliefs. Think of the foundational core values that your business needs to align with your personal beliefs.

_____

_____

_____

What personality traits best describe your business? These can be different than *your* personality traits. Think of them as the personality traits of your business operations.

_____

_____

_____

How do your customers see the values and personality of your business? Think of customer testimonials and reviews. How do your customers perceive your business?

_____

_____

_____

Your business is an entity that has its own future. Can you envision where you want your business to be as it grows up and matures? What does your business look like at its peak of success? Think of terms in employee size, revenue, customers, products, services, and offerings.

_____

_____

_____

_____

What is your vision of success within your business and industry? Think beyond sales and consider other factors, such as how you would like to deliver your expertise and knowledge to clients. For example, successful speaking engagement, online courses, teaching, and books.

_____

_____

_____

_____

NOW PULL IT ALL TOGETHER

How does your business and what you offer give meaning to your life?

_____

_____

_____

How does that align with your moral compass?

_____

_____

_____

_____

STAND OUT FROM YOUR COMPETITORS

You are not your competition. It's key you know why and how you are different. By analyzing your potential client's other options, you will discover how you are distinct. Your competitors are a piece of the conversation that your clients hear. Listen to what they hear. See what they see. Once you do this, you can communicate what is unique about you and your services with distinction, relevance, and value.

RESEARCH YOUR COMPETITORS EXERCISE

Your competitors don't serve your clients the same way as you do. Learning how their offerings are different from yours can reveal better insights into who your ideal clients are and what makes you best for them. Also, what you like and don't like about your competitors' values are key factors in what makes you distinct.

Research your industry. Find a few national big dogs and a few local competitors that do something similar and review their digital footprint.

What social media do they actively use?

_____

_____

_____

How do they engage their followers on social media?

_____

_____

_____

How do they promote engagement from their website?

_____

_____

_____

What do they do or say to be distinct?

_____

_____

_____

How do you see yourself as different from them?

_____

_____

_____

NATIONAL COMPETITORS LIST AND ANALYSIS

List your national competitors' names and websites.

_____

_____

_____

_____

What makes you consider the above list of businesses direct competitors to your offerings?

_____

_____

_____

_____

Review your listed competitors. What are some notable things you can identify about them, such as their target audience and their primary messaging?

_____

_____

_____

_____

Can you identify areas, topics, and industry beliefs, in which you are distinctly different from your competitors?

_____

_____

_____

_____

What is your competitive edge? What makes your business better than your competitors for your audience?

_____

_____

_____

_____

LOCAL COMPETITORS LIST AND ANALYSIS

List your local competitors' names and websites.

_____

_____

_____

_____

What makes you consider the above list of businesses a direct competitor to your offerings?

_____

_____

_____

_____

Review your listed competitors. What are some notable things you can identify about them, such as their target audience and their primary messaging?

_____

_____

_____

_____

Can you identify areas, topics, and industry beliefs in which you are distinctly different than your competitors?

_____

_____

_____

_____

What is your competitive edge? What makes your business better than your competitors for your audience?

_____

_____

_____

_____

SUMMARIZE YOUR INSIGHTS

Review your industry locally and nationally to find the options that your clients see and hear.

Identify how your offerings are uniquely different than your competitors. List at least three things that you see make your offerings different.

_____

_____

_____

Identify how you are uniquely better for your clients than your competitors. List at least three benefits your clients get when working with you that they may not get when working with your competitors.

_____

_____

_____

What are the main strengths of your business? Think operations, delivery, experience.

_____

_____

_____

List aspects of your business that make your offerings strong, unique, and better.

_____

_____

_____

What misinformation does your industry put out there that doesn't serve your clients' success?

_____

_____

_____

How can you "do damage control" and address this misinformation with potential clients?

_____

_____

_____

What industry information do you see that doesn't align with your industry perspective?

_____

_____

_____

NOW PULL IT ALL TOGETHER

What can you do to further distinguish your business from your competitors?

_____

_____

_____

How can you take these tasks one step further to stand distinct and unique in your industry?

_____

_____

_____

chapter three

The Experience is Everything

Regardless of the brand you are building, the people who do business on your behalf have the potential to change how your clients perceive your brand.

Case in point. Buying a car is a process. Most people don't wake up one day and simply decide to buy a car. We recognize we need a new car, review the new features that are popular, and look over our favorite brands and models. We need to get a sense of what we want to buy. However, there's also an emotional piece that weighs into the buying decision as much as the practical side—maybe more. Buying a new car is a great example of this.

I'll never forget the experience my husband Andy and I had when buying a new car. It was going to be primarily his vehicle, so he started researching. He settled on a Subaru and wanted to check it out in person after extensive online research. We both wanted to see how it looked and sit in it to get a sense of how we felt about the model. We weren't particularly ready for a test drive. It was most important at this stage to make sure that the car *felt* right to us.

We found a local Subaru dealer a few miles away, and we went together on a field trip. We were excited to see the new cars, the features, the new designs, and colors. When we got there, a salesman approached us, and we told them we were only looking. He left us to wander around the lot, looking at the models, peaking in, opening doors, viewing the dashboard, testing the seats, and considering how we felt sitting inside the car.

Another salesman approached us. Again, we politely told him we were just looking. Suddenly, unexpectedly, he began to berate us and tell us what we needed to do next—how we needed to take the car on a test drive and experience how it drove. His tone was belligerent and impolite. I stepped back, surprised at the salesman's unexpected anger at us. Andy again told him, no, and they argued for few minutes before the salesman left us alone.

The salesman had spoiled the fun we were having, and we no longer wanted to look at cars. We had accomplished most of what we came out to do, but our fun had been disrupted, so we left.

Andy then did more research and found a dealership about an hour away. This time there was a salesman who listened to us. We happily drove that hour to do business with someone who made us feel comfortable.

The lesson here is that people do business with people—not with organizations. They take their business to someone they trust to treat them well and deliver the goods.

How do you measure up? Are you the professional who treats clients well and delivers what you promise? More importantly, how does your brand communicate how you measure up?

MEASURING YOUR BRAND: KEY METRICS

Your clients are attracted to what they need, wrapped within an experience they enjoy. Your message, how you use words, and the way your visuals look provide insight into the experience you offer. The right look, the right words, the right feel—all must be in alignment with your potential clients for them to choose you. This requires a solid plan.

The key word here is intention. You can't build or create something without a blueprint or plan. Without a map, you are a wanderer who is not in charge of your destiny. Intentionally looking at where you are now and where you want to be in the future helps identify gaps that need work. By understanding what you are aiming for, you can create the path to get there. From starting on the right platform to repositioning your business in your industry, it all starts with a plan of action.

There are two sets of key metrics I use to analyze the effectiveness of a brand:

- External key metrics measure how the world perceives your business.

· Internal key metrics measure elements you can control and have the power to modify or change.

After assessing and understanding how the world sees your brand, you can review the internal key metrics to see how you can shift and change that perception as needed.

I consult with clients launching social media campaigns to drive traffic to their websites. Clients are always fascinated when I review the digital analytics of their websites. Analytics are complex tools that require insight and understanding to learn what is being done right with the online experience you offer—and what can be improved.

Before investing in a promotional or improvement campaign, it's essential to assess the foundation of your brand—how the world perceives your business. Then you can ensure that the pieces you can control are optimized for the best visitor engagement with potential clients. Thoroughly evaluating your brand before investing time and money into campaigns will help ensure your best visitor engagement and return on investment.

EXTERNAL BRAND KEY METRICS

Your brand is what your clients perceive it to be. Do you have a clear image and measurement of your brand and how others see your business?

Your external brand key metrics consist of three things: your offerings, the clients you attract, and the reputation of your business. These three pieces make up how your business is perceived. It's important to evaluate these three metrics and how they relate to your goals when considering future growth.

Let's identify where you stand now and what possibly needs more work.

YOUR OFFERINGS

Make a list of your offerings.

_____

_____

_____

_____

Identify your most popular offering.

_____

_____

Which offering is your favorite to provide or the most enjoyable for you to deliver?

_____

_____

Which offering is your biggest moneymaker?

_____

_____

YOUR CLIENTS

Make a list of your favorite clients.

_____

_____

_____

What is the common thread between these clients?

_____

_____

_____

What makes them so easy to work with?

_____

_____

_____

Make a list of those clients you do not want to work with.

_____

_____

_____

What is the common thread between clients you don't want to serve?

_____

_____

_____

What makes them difficult to work with?

_____
_____
_____

YOUR REPUTATION

What do your clients say about you and your offerings?
Think about client testimonials or what clients say when
referring business to you.

_____
_____
_____

How do you want your business to be seen?

_____
_____
_____

What do you want your business to be known for?

_____
_____
_____

Customer service is vital to crafting your business reputation and perception. What are the foundational pieces that make up your customer service policy?

_____

_____

_____

Does your current customer service policy take into account how you want to be perceived?

_____

_____

_____

INTERNAL BRAND KEY METRICS: TAKE CONTROL OF YOUR BRAND

Above, we looked at the outside view of your brand, how the public and your clients see your business. In the next section, we'll look at the parts of your brand you can control. This section addresses how to influence the public's perception of your business to better align with the brand you want to deliver.

There are four essential elements to executing a solid brand. All four parts make up the internal structure of your brand. This assessment evaluates these four elements and provides a guideline of where your brand needs work.

The four essential elements are:

- Brand Building Basics assesses how clearly you communicate the foundation and basics of your brand through images, visuals, and written content.

- Marketing Foundation Basics assesses how well you capture the attention of your visitors, engage with potential clients, and show clients the true value of working with you.

- Design for Growth assesses how well you adhere to web design trends. This is key to ensuring your visitors are engaged with your message and stay on your website to learn more about you and your business.

- Technology assesses how well you utilize technology standards to ensure you aren't left behind.

BRAND BUILDING BASICS EXERCISE

Your ability to communicate what you stand for clearly and consistently is key to building a strong memorable brand. This exercise will help you define your brand and how you communicate it.

What does your brand stand for?

_____

_____

_____

_____

What are the values behind your business?

_____

_____

_____

_____

What information or resources do you offer your online
visitors to engage with your business?

_____

_____

_____

_____

How is your business different and better for your clients?

_____

_____

_____

_____

Do the photos on your site represent you and your
business?

_____

_____

Do you effectively tell your business story?

_____

_____

MARKETING FOUNDATION BASICS EXERCISE

Marketing connects your potential clients to the information they are looking for. Your digital brand should build the concept of "know, like and trust." If done successfully, potential clients know that you are the expert they are seeking, like you, and trust you have the answers to their questions.

This exercise will help you assess how effectively you are marketing your business using digital tools and trends.

Who are your ideal clients?

_____

_____

_____

_____

Do potential "ideal clients" engage with your business?

_____

_____

Do you use landing pages to build your email list?

_____

_____

What resources do you provide to answer questions during your potential clients' buying process?

_____

_____

_____

_____

Do you connect a Customer Relationship Management tool (CRM) to your website to capture lead information as people engage?

_____

_____

Is the look of your marketing consistent through digital and print?

_____

_____

Do you offer testimonials, case studies, or other ways to establish trust?

_____

_____

DESIGN FOR THE FUTURE CHECKLIST

You've been to that outdated website, the one that you saw and immediately clicked the back button. It's the one that didn't look modern, user-friendly, trendy, or "right." Designing for the future means you are using modern design trends and displaying current information in a standard, logical way. It makes it easy for your website visitors to stay on your site because they don't need to think about how to find the information they are looking for.

This exercise will assess how up-to-date the content and design are on your website.

Does your website reflect your current offerings?

_____

_____

Is the information on your website up to date?

_____

_____

Is the information on your website easily found?

_____

_____

Do you offer articles, blog posts, podcast, or videos to show your expertise?

_____

_____

Is your website designed with the latest trends and standards?

_____

_____

Is it easy to navigate?

_____

_____

TECHNOLOGY CHECKLIST

Technology isn't sexy, but it is the foundation of your digital brand. Effectively managing and wielding it is essential to successful branding. In fact, Google expects websites to be presented in a particular way and will rank your website poorly if it isn't up to snuff.

This exercise will uncover what kinds of website technology you may be lacking to compete in today's highly competitive online world.

Do you know where your domain name is hosted? Your domain name is the foundation of your digital brand. It needs to be in an account that is owned and managed by you, the business owner.

_____

_____

Is your site optimized for viewing on smartphones and tablets? When your site is mobile friendly, the content adjusts and optimizes how the information is displayed when viewing on various devices, like a smartphone or tablet.

_____

_____

Do you use an SSL certificate (HTTPS)? It's highly recommended all websites use HTTPS to browse your website pages securely.

_____

_____

Do you have a website backup plan in place? Building your website was an investment in your business. Backing up your website is crucial to keeping this investment safe.

_____

_____

Do you have Google Analytics and Search Console accounts? Google measures the traffic coming to your site and provides insights into how your web pages are being used.

_____

_____

Is your business listed on Google Maps? If you have a brick-and-mortar storefront, you should have your business listed on Google Maps.

_____

_____

Do you have a Google My Business account? Google allows you to create a business listing and manage the public profile.

_____

_____

Do you have proper on-page search engine optimization? This is the basic metadata for how your website shows up on the search engine results page.

_____

_____

chapter four

The Journey to Your Ideal Client

Do you remember the yellow pages? They used to be the primary way people learned about businesses. The ads were simple, and it was a challenge to fit what you needed to say in the small amount of space you could afford. That space needed to target what you did in the simplest, quickest way. Usually, the ads communicated what a business sold and included a little bit about why the service or product was valuable. It was hard to say much in that small space.

At that time, businesses also relied on other ways for people to hear about them. Marketing was wide. It crossed many printed mediums and the airwaves, radio, and television, to make customers aware of businesses. The goal of marketing was to get in front of the customers, so they would learn your business's name, look it up in the yellow pages, and call. In addition, businesses were organized by category, so it was easy for customers to find what they needed, even if they did not know a business's name. If a business wasn't in the local yellow pages, it would be difficult to find its phone number—or even know that it existed. Marketing was different and simpler in many ways.

Now, the rules have changed, the way we market has changed, and so has the way we communicate. Social media has forever altered the landscape of how we create and stand out in our business relationships. In today's digital world, millions of other businesses are doing the same thing we do, so it's critical to get noticed.

The days of one-sided marketing have come to an end. Marketing has evolved into a multimedia, two-sided conversation with your clients. That connection is created when you craft a brand that personifies your business, values, and voice. It's the glue that holds together your online and offline customer experience, your internal work ethic, and your interaction with your clients. It's the bridge that connects your purpose to your customers' struggles. In essence, your brand comes to life as a multichannel conversation that builds and connects with your tribe.

Customer-centric design is an art that requires a deep understanding of your tribe of ideal clients. It starts with knowing who your perfect clients are and stepping into their shoes to see what information they need. This is key to connecting with them through multi-channel conversations.

Customer-centric design is focused on creating an exceptional customer experience for your ideal clients: from beginning to end, from online to offline. It's providing your services with the intention of making your clients feel great when doing business with you.

CONNECT WITH YOUR IDEAL CLIENT

Connection. It's the single most important piece of building a strong business. It includes knowing your tribe, finding your tribe, and connecting with your tribe. Connection has been the overarching element of success in my business.

Once I had decided to venture out on my own as an entrepreneur, I realized I didn't know who I specifically wanted to serve. I only knew one thing – that I wanted to help small businesses. I wanted to get them online so they would have a chance to make an impact in their community.

At the time, social media was blazing onto the scene. Facebook had just opened to the public in the fall of 2006. It was a whole new world to those that had been in business for a while. Social media was like a new set of foreign tools that didn't operate the same as the old set of tools. For many business owners, this was an alien way to do business. They were used to meeting in person and connecting through a handshake over a meal. That was changing, and I saw the reality of that.

Websites and the way business owners were communicating to the world were forever influenced by social media and the way we connected there. Websites that were simply lists of services, with no heart and soul, mirroring a brochure or yellow page ad, no longer worked. The website was being redefined as a digital platform and the very heartbeat of marketing a business. Adapting to this revolution was a tall order for those who thought their brick-and-mortar building was the heart of their businesses. Brick-and-mortar *was* the heart of business—until it wasn't.

With the demise of the yellow pages, the most convenient way to find a business became searching online and finding a website—and not just any website. Today, your website has to be your digital marketplace, your digital brick-and-mortar. It has to capture the essence of what makes you different.

The rules have also changed. The website has become a tool for potential customers to learn more about you and your business. This wasn't always the way it worked in advertising—small businesses with limited budgets simply stated what they did in local print ads and let customers pick up the phone to call.

On the other hand, large corporations with huge marketing budgets have been producing effective advertising to brand themselves for decades. Think of the memorable and highly effective advertising and branding campaigns of cigarettes, alcohol, and cars of the '60s through the '80s. For example:

"You've come a long way baby" (Virginia Slims cigarettes)
"It's Miller time" (Miller beer)
"Go topless this summer" (Triumph Spitfire convertible)

Imagine the experiences these words promised—and countless consumers bought it. They may have loved the products, but it was the branding that connected and hooked them emotionally to big companies.

This kind of branding was only available to the "big guys" until recently. Today websites and social media marketing allow entrepreneurs and small businesses to grab a piece of the pie that was untouchable in the past. Even the little guy with a limited budget can brand himself as well as big corporations—maybe better.

If you want to engage with your ideal clients, you need to think of your website, and the words, images, and offerings on it, as a reference for your clients. It needs to be a place where they can learn from your industry experience, and it should provide answers to their questions. Most of all, it must have the heart and soul that your ideal clients connect to.

Your brand is critical to connecting with your ideal client, and your website and digital presence needs to work as hard as you do to make this happen. It starts with stepping into the shoes of your clients. Get into their mindset and learn what you can about them and their journey. Then craft a journey to *their* success or happiness.

MARKET TO YOUR IDEAL CLIENT

In marketing today there's a saying, "You can't please everyone." When creating beautiful brands, this saying comes into play in a big way. There is no way that a single website can appeal to every market, every demographic, and every region. Your ability to niche your clients into small groups facilitates your ability to have your content speak directly to them.

Niche groups of clients or customers can be specific to an industry, such as healthcare, or to an individual entrepreneur or service-based business, such as business coaches and authors. They can also be specific to a certain-sized business (for example, one to three employees or been in business more than three years).

Your content needs to speak directly to your niche audience. It should employ words and images that help them identify themselves and know that you are right for them. You should also use the same language they use to discuss the problems or needs that your business can address.

I know you've run across this before. You land on a web page that is too general or not written with your issue in mind. Maybe it's not written personally enough for you to care to read on. What happens? You move on.

When you target everyone with your social media and website, when you are not specific enough, you risk being viewed as a commodity. When that happens, the only factor that differentiates you is price. You don't want price point to be where your clients are focused. You want your clients to know specifically who you work with and who you help. You need to write killer content and provide images that make them feel you are the right solution for them.

GROUP CLIENTS INTO BUCKETS

When identifying your ideal client, understand there are multiple groups or "buckets" of clients that you might serve. The smaller you can make these buckets, the more targeted you can be in attracting the right group and making meaningful connections with them.

Here is an example of grouping your clients into buckets. Kimberly Alexander Inc. is a growth strategist. She provides business coaching to women entrepreneurs who know they are meant to do big things. She serves these purpose-driven women entrepreneurs at multiple points during their business growth journey. Her audience can be represented as two niche groups:

- She serves women entrepreneurs that have been struggling and need to establish a business foundation.
- She helps established women business owners create programs to grow their business beyond six figures.

The distinction between the groups is where they are in their business growth. Depending upon their journey, she has specific ways to serve that niche audience.

As another example, CR Conversations provides sales training to entrepreneurs and small businesses. CEO Katie Myers provides a specific product for a specific client group. One product is The Conversation Club, an online membership offering. It includes group sales training videos, online group masterminding on sales techniques, and support and resources exclusive to her members.

Myers' clients struggle with sales and are not natural salespeople. The training she offers is for a small group of entrepreneurs who are typically running their business by themselves as a solopreneur. They have started their businesses for the freedom and lifestyle, and have a strong desire to change the lives of their clients. Katie's training techniques and style is specific to these women entrepreneurs. Her clients seek her out because she speaks directly to the challenges of a purpose-driven, solo-business owner who is not a natural salesperson and is struggling to increase sales.

Both examples show how you can tailor your offerings to a very specific group or niche of clients and their needs. Knowing and understanding their struggles will help you craft a marketing message that speaks directly to individuals. They, in turn, will connect and know that your offerings address their specific situation.

Now that you're in the mindset of thinking of your clients in a niche way, you are ready to think about their journeys. That includes their experiences, issues, or needs that have led them to seek your solution. Their journeys are important for you to understand because they will provide deeper insight into your ideal client.

IDENTIFY AND UNDERSTAND YOUR IDEAL CLIENT

The following exercise is to help you identify your ideal client groups and show your understanding of their journeys to working with you. This includes understanding their problems, frustrations, and failings before reaching out to you.

Understand Your Ideal Client Exercise

Think of your ideal clients as a group that has the best characteristics that you identified in the External Brand Key Metrics "Understand Your Clients" exercise in chapter three. Think of them as two or three distinct groups of clients you want to work with. Identify the ideal client traits of each group.

_____

_____

_____

_____

What makes your ideal clients ideal? In other words, why do you want to work with them, or what makes it easy to work with them? Be clear in this. For example, is it how they find you, their struggle, or their personality and approach? Is it their experience or mindset?

_____

_____

_____

_____

Sometimes our ideal clients are "difficult" in some ways. For example, they may question things, which can mean they are insightful. List a few qualities or traits that you may not initially like in an ideal client but makes them easier to work within the long run.

_____

_____

_____

_____

_____

_____

_____

_____

It's just as important to recognize who you don't want to work with as knowing who you do want to work with. Identify the clients you don't want to work with. Which clients have you worked with who didn't get your methods or connect with your purpose? Who has worked against your processes or is not of the same mind as you are? Identify those people here. Then make sure that you are intentional with your marketing and messaging to NOT attract them.

_____

_____

_____

_____

_____

_____

_____

_____

SUMMARIZE WHAT YOU LEARNED

What values are important to your clients when seeking out your services or offerings? Examples include trustworthy, fun, honesty, and dependability.

_____

_____

_____

_____

What elements do they feel are important or non-negotiable in the delivery of your services or offerings? Examples are responsiveness, transparency.

_____

_____

_____

_____

YOUR IDEAL CLIENT JOURNEY EXERCISE

Your clients go through a journey before they reach you. Sometimes they have worked with the wrong people and present as distrusting of you because of those past experiences. They may also come to you with high expectations because of who they worked with in the past. Either way, the more you understand about their past, their mindset, and perspective, the better you can communicate to them your process, your values, and what they can expect.

The above exercise helped you to understand your ideal clients better. Now I want you to use what you have learned to create a clear picture of your ideal client's persona. Creating this persona is a way of consolidating your ideal clients into a single sample client.

This exercise is the foundation of building a solid, memorable brand. When completing this worksheet, you may consolidate the traits of actual clients, or you may use traits you want to attract. Remember that clients are real people and real customers. Never lose sight of the fact that they are the most important people to your business.

THE IDEAL CLIENT JOURNEY

Name: _____

Age Group: _____

Occupation or Industry: _____

Marital and family status: _____

Location or Demographic: _____

Needs or Problems Your Ideal Client Wants Resolved

List the basic needs or problem(s) your ideal client wants resolved.

_____

_____

_____

_____

Underlying Challenges

What is the primary challenge your ideal client faces because of the set of issues you just listed above?

_____

_____

_____

_____

The Final Outcome

What is your ideal client's perfect world?

_____

_____

_____

_____

What is your ideal client's vision of what it would be like if the problem was resolved?

_____

_____

_____

_____

Incentives to Succeed

What incentivizes your ideal client to see a successful outcome?

_____

_____

_____

_____

What inspires him or her to move forward?

_____

_____

_____

_____

What is your ideal client's personal or business goals that motivate him or her to take action?

_____

_____

_____

_____

Journey to You

What is your ideal client's background and past experiences?

_____

_____

_____

_____

Summarize their journey to you.

_____

_____

_____

_____

Values to Finding a Solution

What is your ideal client looking for in a service provider? Examples include fun, excitement, getting the job done, timeliness, efficiency, and cost.

_____

_____

_____

What's Holding Your Ideal Client Back?

_____

_____

_____

_____

What are your ideal client's main frustrations or feelings surrounding his/her challenge?

_____

_____

_____

_____

What is holding your ideal client back from seeking a solution? Example include funding, time, uncertainty.

_____

_____

_____
_____

Identify the Tipping Point

At what point does your ideal client seek services?

_____
_____
_____
_____

What forces their hand to take action?

_____
_____
_____

SUMMARIZE WHAT YOU LEARNED

Brainstorm words that express how your ideal client will feel when his/her problems are fixed.

_____
_____
_____
_____

What is your ideal client looking forward to?

_____

_____

_____

_____

What is the right outcome?

_____

_____

_____

_____

What does your ideal client's life look like when his/her problems are solved?

_____

_____

_____

_____

How can you change your messaging or service delivery to let your ideal client know that you understand their journey?

_____

_____

_____

_____

chapter five

Embracing Your Superpower

I have always made it a point to be friendly with people in my industry. There's no use being competitive because I know I am different than my competition. People choose to work with me because of who I am, my approach to things, and my personality.

I remember a conversation with a marketing director for another web design company. It started friendly enough. Then he asked me what my differentiating factor was—what made me different and distinct. I answered, "ME!"

I told him that I made my business distinct with my personality, approach, and perspective. I was the one thing that made my business unique.

I distinctly remember his response: "Everyone says that!"

That stopped the conversation. At that time, I couldn't

put into words what was so different about me. It took self-exploration and insight to see what it was that made me distinct from my industry counterparts.

That response from that marketing director was the start of my journey to transform my web design business into a brand-building business. First, I had to prove to *myself* that I was unique, and I had to discover and understand what I was doing differently from my competitors. Then I had to express and demonstrate these things to others.

All successful entrepreneurs must do the same thing, but it takes more than just saying it to make it real. We must put our finger on what we do differently from our competitors. Is it how we operate and how we treat our customers? Is it how we approach our offerings?

Discovering the answers is the key to learning your true power—your superpower. Your superpower also includes your life experience, industry expertise, accreditations, degrees, passion, and purpose. All these things give you the right to be the expert you are destined to be.

Each of us has greatness inside. We all have a superpower. It's up to us to recognize it, show confidence in our expertise, and boldly present it to the world.

FINDING THE COURAGE TO STEP INTO YOUR SUPERPOWER

To step into your superpower and make the impact you want to make in this world, you must be comfortable with fear. This isn't about being fearless—it's about having courage. It's being afraid and moving forward anyway. It's feeling fear and not standing still or moving backwards. Courage to move forward. Action despite fear. The true definition of fearless is courage.

So, how do you embrace your fear and find your courage? Begin by understanding you're not perfect, nor are you meant to be. It's OK to be messy. It's OK to step outside your comfort zone try something new and to do it imperfectly. It's OK to make a mistake and try it again. Not only are these things OK, but they are also a necessary part of stepping into your superpower.

We've all heard the saying, "Fake it 'til you make it." That cliché may mimic courage, but if you don't actually step into that space of fear, you aren't learning what it takes to be better. Allow yourself to be vulnerable and embrace the small wins. I don't want you to "Fake it 'til you make it." I want you to embrace your messy and do it your way.

For me, finding courage came from strapping my feet to a five-foot snowboard and learning to carve down a steep mountain. It came from doing something that was far outside my comfort zone and embracing the sport until I owned it.

It was through teaching myself to snowboard that I learned to trust in myself and not feed into fear. Snowboarding is a painful sport to learn. You often clip the front edge of your board and face-plant into the snow when beginning to carve. For me, it took a long time to learn the art of leaning into the edge with just the right amount of weight and then shifting on the board to begin the switch to the other edge. I found that my fear was holding me back from mastering the technique. I would hesitate in shifting my weight at the moment I needed it most, and I would crash face first in the snow.

What I realized is that if I didn't overthink and focused solely on feeling the way the board moved underneath me, I knew what I needed to do. By shutting down the logical part of my brain, and trusting in the movements and the flow, I was able to master the sport. I learned to feel courage and came to trust in my skills. Now, I take that experience into my life whenever I need to step into fear to grow and learn.

I also embraced my fears in the business world. In my early days, I was afraid of public speaking and knew I was not good at it, but I signed up to speak anyway. I took speaking and leadership roles as they came to me, presenting to groups as I was asked. I welcomed any excuse to get up in front of an audience. It taught me to embrace the jitters and the butterflies. I had to expect that my brain would sometimes stop in the middle of a sentence, and I learned to laugh it off and move on.

These experiences taught me not to focus on my weaknesses but on what I could control and what I was brilliant at. I learned to accept that my heart was beating in my throat and to smile at the audience and tell them how this was hard for me to overcome. I discovered that this endeared me to them—and more importantly, it allowed me to feel connected to them. I found that once I was connected to them, I could be more authentic and relax.

I learned that I'm not a polished public speaker, but I'm gifted with connecting, telling stories, and getting the audience to engage with me. I realized that's because I feel more comfortable with a conversation than a formal speech. I speak from the heart with emotion. By doing that again and again and pushing myself outside my comfort zone, I discovered my gifts and made my way through a self-imposed, terrifying and trackless forest.

Finding your courage is just that. It's doing something that scares you again and again until you find the path that takes you to an island of light within the dark forest. It's breaking through how you think it's supposed to be done and finding your way to make it happen.

We often see ourselves through a lens of what we think we are supposed to be. Once we break free of those self-imposed expectations, we find that we were brave all along. We had the answers within us, but our fear did not allow us to see our potential.

It's not easy to be a business owner, run a business, and embrace the impact you were meant to make on this earth. That is scary stuff. You might be halfway there, running your business, but not quite ready to embrace your story. You might hesitate to embrace full vulnerability and announce to the world what you have to offer.

If that describes you, you must first accept that your fear is holding you back. True success, joy, and meaning are on the other side of fear. Let it go and trust yourself. You have the answers you need already. You need to have that faith, see the path, and take the first step.

Believing in yourself is not scary. Believing in yourself so strongly that you define yourself as a brand and a public fig-ure is terrifying. It's easy to say what you do and rattle off a list of services you offer. It's even easy to say why potential clients need you. What's not easy is saying it in a way that expresses your vulnerability. This is being authentic and honoring the journey that brought you to where you are.

I know that everyone has a history. Let's call it the baggage you carry that you may not be proud of. We all have fallen and stood again, dusting ourselves off and moving forward. That is what has made us stronger and better—the mistakes we make and what we learn from them.

Finding your superpower means embracing your messy story. Recognize your talents and gifts and acknowledge your weaknesses—but don't focus on them. Remember that you don't have to have it all figured out right away, but you do need to have faith in yourself and know you'll find the answers when you need them.

You're the Expert Exercise

In this exercise list all the things that make you the expert in what you do. List life experiences, industry experience, accreditations, and degrees. Write about how your business connects to your purpose and passion.

You are an expert in your industry and business. What gives you the right to be called an expert?

_____

_____

_____

_____

List life experiences.

_____

_____

_____

_____

List industry experiences.

_____

_____

_____

_____

List what you are passionate about as it pertains to your business.

_____

_____

_____

_____

What experience or event has made you a topic expert?

_____

_____

_____

_____

List challenges that you needed to overcome. Examples include public speaking and learning new technology.

_____

_____

_____

_____

What challenges are you currently looking to overcome that can enhance your impact? Think of steps you can take toward overcoming those challenges. List steps that are manageable and not too overwhelming.

_____

_____

_____

_____

Write about how you can use your expertise or experience to feel more confident in areas outside your comfort zone.

_____

_____

_____

_____

Harness Your Superpower Exercise

Success is a journey. It's not something that comes to you, but something that you actively make happen.

Believe in Yourself

Your belief in yourself is the fuel to your superpower.

I dare you to dream. What does a successful life look like to you?

_____

_____

_____

_____

In that life, what do you see you need to do or be to make that possible?

_____

_____

_____

_____

Sometimes we stand in our own way or are held back by our fears. What holds you back from seeing or reaching your full potential?

_____

_____

_____

_____

Each day we make a choice to either step into our challenges, or not. Taking that step moves us closer to our version of success. What stops you from really owning your power?

_____

_____

_____

_____

Value Your Talents, Gifts, and Knowledge

You are worthy of the success that lies in front of you.

List your strengths or talents that have contributed to your business success.

_____

_____

_____

_____

How do you use your strengths in your business?

_____

_____

_____

_____

What you do impacts the world. Understanding that gives you fuel to do it again. How does your expertise and knowledge change the lives of your clients?

_____

_____

_____

_____

Be Willing to Do the Hard Work

You are committed to being the best you can be.

What challenges have you needed to push through to be where you are today?

_____

_____

_____

_____

Success only comes when we continually better ourselves. What are you currently struggling with or need to obtain to push into the next level?

_____

_____

_____

_____

What inspires you each day to do what you do? How can this inspiration be used to work through your current challenges?

_____

_____

_____

_____

Small steps get you to success faster than no forward motion at all. Create a plan of small doable steps that you can do to get you closer to success.

_____

_____

_____

_____

chapter six

Defining Your Purpose

You are what is unique and different about your business. So how do you capture your uniqueness in your brand story? Your brand story should speak to your purpose, your mission in life, and your values and culture. It builds the bridge between your purpose and your client's challenges. Told right, it conveys to your clients that you are the one that "gets" them and will help them solve their problems.

Your brand story should speak from your heart, telling the tale of your journey and how you arrived where you are today. It should be short and sweet, memorable and simple. But it isn't just a random story. It speaks about your values and the transformation you went through. Your brand story is a way for your potential clients to glimpse into your soul and see your voyage into your purpose. Quite a challenge for a simple story.

Finding the pieces of your brand story starts with identifying the core of your superpower—through the three non-negotiables of success. By coming back to those and seeing how they apply to you and your journey, you'll see where you are today and how to communicate your story.

What's Your Purpose Exercise

Believe in Yourself

Your belief in yourself is foundational to your story. Consider how you needed to transform and the lessons you learned to stand in your brilliance. This is the start of your story.

Think back to your breakthrough to success. When did you step into and own who you are? What life events led you to step into your expertise and commit to making an impact?

_____

_____

_____

_____

What did you need to conquer to stand in your brilliance? Think mindset or other hurdles that you saw were stopping you from stepping forward.

_____

_____

_____

_____

What did you need to learn and do to move forward? I want you to identify the transformation you experienced when you stepped into believing in yourself.

_____

_____

_____

_____

Value Your Talent, Gifts, and Knowledge

You bring value to your business. Your talents and gifts are unique to you. They can be learned skills, or they might be life lessons that propelled you to where you are today. These lessons and skills are the values you bring to your business and the ones that help build your moral compass and foundation to your brand story.

I invite you to dream and fully accept who you are. What could you accomplish if you had more time, money, education, resources, etc.?

_____

_____

_____

_____

Just as important as learning your strengths, is acknowledging your weaknesses and what you can let go of to step into your superpower. List things that drain your energy and stop you from achieving your potential.

_____

_____

_____

_____

Communicating your value lies in showing your experience and expertise. List your credentials. Include awards, degrees, accreditations, and life lessons that make you the expert in what you do.

_____

_____

_____

_____

Be Willing to Do the Hard Work

Success is not easy. It takes work, persistence, and consistent desire to move forward to fulfill your dream. Success is paved with the work you put into the journey.

To be successful, you need to step outside your comfort zone. What have you needed to learn or do that wasn't easy and took you outside your comfort zone?

_____

_____

_____

_____

Look into your process of how you made that transition. What inspired you through the process? In other words, what was your motivation to move towards success?

_____

_____

_____

_____

Sometimes we perceive a challenge as something that stops us or forces us to move in another direction. Challenges should be viewed not as obstacles but as a way to prove that we have what it takes to succeed. What challenges or life events did you need to conquer to continue on your path to success?

_____

_____

_____

_____

What underlying factor drives you to work so hard to accomplish your goals?

_____

_____

_____

_____

What lessons have you learned that have contributed to your journey?

_____

_____

_____

_____

ELEMENTS OF YOUR STORY

Your story needs to convey the heart and soul of what brought you to where you are. It should:

- Communicate the lessons you have learned.
- Show the value you bring to your clients.
- Hint at your values and what is important to you.
- Exemplify the purpose of what you do.

That's a tall order. Read through your answers in the exercise above and condense what you've brainstormed to find the key elements of your brand story.

- Identify your transformation or lessons learned.
- Identify life events that propelled you through your transformation.
- What life events moved you outside your comfort zone and brought you closer to your success?
- Identify one or two powerful challenges that made you who you are today.

- What life events helped you identify your purpose? Your purpose is what drives you to move forward each day. It can be tangible or intangible and be derived from your past experiences or something you are working towards.

CREATE A CULTURE WITH YOUR VALUES

Growing a successful company means bringing people into the business, including vendors, assistants, and employees. How can you grow past being a solopreneur into a larger business model that maintains your values and vision? You create a culture that fosters growth and connects with what is important to you and your clients.

A company culture consists of values. Values that mean something to you and your clients should also mean something to your business. By defining your values and aligning them with the values of your ideal client, you create the foundation for a culture. That culture is a critical underpinning of your vendors, your team, and your brand. Everyone who works on behalf of your business must exude the same values and level of integrity.

BUSINESS CULTURE EXAMPLE: BLUE ZENITH

Below is the list of values of Blue Zenith culture. In it, I've defined the values that are important to me and operating my business. More important are the values that my clients expect from me. In defining them and the Blue Zenith culture so precisely, I show my employees what is expected of them when working with clients or as a team. These values guide and integrate my team into being a part of the Blue Zenith culture.

Notice how I define each value as it relates to Blue Zenith operations and to our customers and interactions with them. It's key to tie your values definitions into what they mean to your business. This creates an effective tool to guide business and hiring decisions and choosing vendors and strategic partners to build a strong team.

At Blue Zenith, we value these traits:

Honesty. I vow to be honest when seeking answers and providing guidance.

- Know what you don't know and seek out answers when needed.
- Be quick to admit mistakes.

Impact. I am dedicated to solving problems and finding impactful solutions.

- Finish the job. Follow through with a job until it's completed.
- Focus on results.

Respect. I will treat people with respect.

- Remain calm during stressful situations and interactions with clients, vendors, and colleagues.
- Keep your exchanges professional even when you do not agree with someone.

Communicate. I will strive to be concise and articulate in all communications. I will listen to understand.

- Not everyone understands what you do. It is important to know who you are talking to and appreciate their perspective.
- Communicate effectively and use clear, concise language that is easy to comprehend.

Curious. I have a strong desire to learn and seek to understand.

- Remain knowledgeable about our industry, our clients, technology and business.

Innovate. Always seek better ways to solve a problem.

- Challenge assumptions when warranted and suggest a better approach.

Courage. I will make tough decisions when needed.

- Question actions inconsistent with our values.
- Take smart risks.

Motivate. I will inspire others by my actions.

- Do the right thing even when people aren't looking.

Positive. I will be a positive team member. I will make time to help others.

Your Values, Your Culture Exercise

This exercise will help define what your brand stands for and what you expect from yourself, your vendors, and employees. It is important that anyone working with you knows what is expected of him or her and how to function in your business. In turn, your customers will have a consistent experience with your business because you have created a consistent value system and business culture.

This exercise will also define values through the eyes of your clients and uncover what is important to them when working with you.

Writing down your values helps define your culture. Use my example above of Blue Zenith values and business culture to inspire your own list of values. Remember that your values need to communicate your business culture and how your clients want to be treated.

At my business, we value these traits:

_____

_____

_____

_____

_____

_____

_____

_____

_____

_____

YOUR BUSINESS CULTURE EXERCISE

In this exercise, you will review the list of values you defined above and give them purpose and meaning to your potential and ideal clients. Take time to write your answers in a way that defines your culture through the eyes of your clients and what they want to experience.

What are your customers looking for when seeking out your services?

_____

_____

_____

_____

How do they want to be treated?

_____

_____

_____

_____

What experience can you provide that would attract them to work with you?

_____

_____

_____

_____

BRAINSTORM YOUR PURPOSE EXERCISE

Do you have a life built around things that give you purpose and joy? You should be living a purposeful life, one that supports your ideals and values. If you aren't, then you aren't living to your potential. To create that life, you need to feel worthy of it. Your business purpose should fulfill your personal purpose and connect with your big why.

Simon Sinek's Ted Talk, "Start with Why," is a must-see to understand the importance of clearly defining your purpose. His talk speaks to how we can differentiate our businesses simply by redefining how we see ourselves in the world. By leading with our purpose, we inspire our clients and connect at a deeper level.

By identifying the purpose that inspires and motivates you in your business, you allow your clients and potential clients to glimpse what drives you. People connect with that. Those that have the same world-view and perspective will align themselves with your purpose and will connect with you on a deeper level. That is why it's so important to showcase your heartfelt purpose in your brand messaging and in how you present yourself to the world.

Think deeply about your purpose and why you chose it. Start with identifying what keeps you going each day—the outcomes that are rewarding your soul.

What is the number one reason that your business exists?

_____

_____

_____

_____

_____

_____

_____

_____

What is its core purpose to your clients' lives?

_____

_____

_____

_____

What is the ultimate difference your business makes in the world?

_____

_____

_____

_____

Identify what your business is meant to do. What is the one accomplishment that would prove that your business is successful?

_____

_____

_____

FINDING MY PURPOSE

It was through the next exercise that I realized the true purpose behind my business. From the beginning, I identified with the entrepreneur and small business. Both my parents had been entrepreneurs, and I understood how their businesses made an honest difference in their community.

I had been a computer developer providing the best solutions to the corporate world. After losing my job, I wanted to provide the same high level of presentation and technology to small businesses. When I focused on the entrepreneur, I knew I had found my tribe. I provided a personal level of service that delivered rapid results. I was making a difference one business at a time. That focus allowed me to drill deeper into understanding the true purpose of my business and its offerings.

Aiden Durham, of 180 Law Co., is a business lawyer like no other. She does not fit the mold of a typical law services business. Though she does provide standard legal services, it's how she markets and delivers her services that makes her unique. Watch her YouTube channel, All Up in Yo' Business, and you will see immediately she is different. She connects with entrepreneurs and small business owners that are looking for honest legal advice.

Developing her digital brand was so much fun. By adding her unique attitude to the content and visual design, it created a brand unlike any other lawyer's and set her offerings apart. When people go to her website now, they see her top and front. Her message is professional—with attitude. You'll see she is unique and friendly and has the lawyer sassiness she needs to get things done. That is who she is and what makes her successful.

DEFINE YOUR PURPOSE

During my journey, I came to understand why it was so important to me to help the entrepreneur. I realized that what drove me to find meaning and purpose stemmed from something deeper, including my childhood experiences.

As a child, I had been bullied for years and told that my voice didn't matter. I had been silenced by not being heard. That experience scared me and inspired compassion for others who were sitting on the sidelines, not feeling part of the crowd. It drove me to be more aware of those who felt the same way as I had. It compelled me to give voice to those who felt invisible. That motivation still drives me today.

My purpose developed from my insecurities, vulnerabilities, and my childhood experiences of feeling invisible and lost. Once I tied together all the disjointed moments in my past, it all made sense. I saw the bigger picture of where I had been pulled (or pushed) in defining my life. Over time, it became my passion to use my talents and gifts to drive small business entrepreneurs to find their voice and fulfill their own dreams and purpose.

This is the journey you need to take to find your passion, your purpose, and what drives you. For me, it drills down to "giving voice." I give voice to entrepreneurs who are inspired to impact their clients and ultimately change the world.

Now, I want you to take your journey by outlining the experiences you feel have defined your life. You may not see the thread of connection right away, but you will eventually discover the nearly invisible string that ties together the most important moments in your life. Know that each one is a significant moment in driving you forward towards your purpose. These life experiences plus your skills give you the tools to fulfill your purpose.

DEFINE YOUR PURPOSE EXERCISE

List your most significant life experiences. These are events that stick out to you and changed you in a big way.

_____

_____

_____

_____

From reviewing these events, what are the life lessons you needed to learn to grow past each challenge? This list will be broad, but something in this list will be a piece of the connecting string. The connecting string is the thread that invisibly links your life experiences to your purpose and meaning.

_____

_____

_____

_____

What effect does your solution make on your client's life? List the benefits that you provide when solving your clients' challenges.

_____

_____

_____

_____

TIE IT ALL TOGETHER

Can you find that nearly invisible string that ties together your life events, your foundational beliefs, and your industry experience? That string is what leads you to your true purpose, your why, and gives meaning to your life and business.

_____

_____

_____

_____

Can you identify the purpose behind your business?

_____

_____

_____

_____

chapter seven

Crafting Your Brand Story

At this point, you may be feeling vulnerable. Your story may be hard for you to tell. The events you listed above speak of challenging times in your life. They tell of your failings, how you stumbled, were afraid, how you made a wrong decision, or where you felt vulnerable and not good enough. From my experience, I know you are not alone. I felt this hesitation myself and sense it from many of my clients.

Think back to my story. It tells of a time that I walked away from a paycheck when my family needed it the most. On the one hand, I felt I let down the most important people in my life. But if I hadn't chosen to value myself and time with my family, I would not be where I am now. That step prepared me to walk into the confidence I needed to start my own business.

Your story needs to be told, not from the place where you are lacking, but from your point of triumph. This story includes how you risked something, lost something, how you stumbled, and most importantly, how you rose up. Life is guaranteed to challenge us. What we must find in those challenges are the lessons that teach us something about our character. That character is what your clients are seeking to provide them with faith and inspiration: If you can do it, so can they.

THE LETTER TO YOUR TRIBE EXERCISE

Writing a letter to your tribe is a thing of beauty. It captures the compassion you feel towards your ideal clients—your tribe. Writing this letter is a simple exercise that I've asked my clients to do for years.

There is nothing more compelling for potential clients than reading that letter from the home page of your website. It speaks from a place of emotion. It captures your compassion and reaches through the screen showing your genuine desire to help them. It also documents your expertise and shows your audience how you will move them forward, away from their current struggles.

Heartfelt passion drives us to fulfill our purpose. When we see someone fail, and we know we can help him or her, it truly touches our heart. That feeling should fuel the letter to your tribe. The letter should communicate how you see their individual successes. By knowing you're the right one to help them meet their challenges, you can convey the fire you have to fulfill your purpose and instill success in their lives.

I now ask you to sit quietly and imagine a potential client who is failing at a goal. Think of a situation for which you know you can offer effective solutions. See yourself take the client by the shoulders, look them squarely in the eyes, and speak to them.

What do you say when he or she is at the lowest point or doesn't yet see where or how failure is occurring?

Your guidance should be what all your potential clients need to hear. Your words should come from the heart and offer confidence, strength, and hope. They also speak of the skills you have that will help them achieve their desired outcome. Those words make up the letter to your tribe. They are the seeds that spring forth from your superpower. I challenge you to sit quietly now, envision this, and write your letter.

Dear Client,

_____

_____

_____

_____

_____

_____

_____

_____

_____

_____

WRITING YOUR BRAND STORY EXERCISE

By the time you've reached this point, you have identified all the pieces of your brand story: your letter to your tribe, your business values and culture, and your purpose. Review those exercises and your answers as you prepare to pull it all together.

Review the Purpose Exercise you completed to find the invisible thread of your purpose. It included listing significant moments in your life that could be the starting point of your brand story.

Now let's consider the basic elements of writing your brand story. For this exercise, list the answers in a few short sentences. Use your answers to remind yourself of the pieces of your brand story.

- The characters: Who are the characters in your story? You will play a prominent role, but there may be others needed to support the story's concepts.
- The challenge: Identify the challenge that you needed to work through.
- The plot. Identify the general plot of your story and how you came to an impactful ending.
- The transformation: Identify the transformation you needed to make. What lesson did you need to learn to work through your challenge?
- The promise: All good brand stories end with a promise that you will deliver the desired outcome. A sincere promise inspires clients to choose you. What is the promise of your story?

_____

_____

_____

_____

_____

_____

_____

_____

_____

_____

_____

_____

_____

_____

_____

_____

_____

_____

_____

_____

_____

_____

_____

_____

_____

_____

CREATING IMPACT IN YOUR BRAND STORY

Your brand story needs to be memorable and make an impact on your business and the way your ideal clients see you. Though your brand story is yours, it needs to be meaningful to those reading or hearing it.

I've been asked about how vulnerable an entrepreneur should be in telling a story. My answer is that you should craft the story from life events. You should choose events that make your story worth listening to and have meaning for your ideal clients. Your story should also be simple and contain only the events that move the story forward.

I've created a guideline of tips to help keep you focused as you write: the acronym IMPACT. To write a brand story with impact it must contain these elements:

I - Inspiration. Your story must inspire your clients, providing them hope for a solution. They need to see that you can show them the path to conquer their struggles and attain transformation.

M - Magnification. Your expertise and values should be the core of your story. They must provide a means to glimpse into your superpower, your purpose, and your values.

P - Perspective. Never lose sight of your audience. Your story should be told in a way that shows you understand your clients' perspectives. It should help them identify their own struggles and provide them with a solution.

A - Action. Every good story is relatable through action, and your clients should see themselves in the story. Told well, your story will draw them into the plot. In the midst of their struggles, clients sometimes only see what is directly in front of them. A good story helps them see the bigger picture and gain personal insight through the story's action.

C - Character. Your story should highlight a challenge in your life and how you handled it. How you handle adversity provides insight into your character. No challenge is too small for a story if the lessons you learned propelled you to another place in your life.

T - Transformation. Your story should highlight a transformative moment in your life. Think about the lessons you learned through conquering your challenges that led to transformation and solved your problems. Your transformation should reflect the transformation that your clients desire.

Now write your first draft of your brand story in five short paragraphs or less. Remember that this will be just a rough, working draft, which you will need to rework and tweak over time. Do not strive for perfection. Allow yourself to be imperfect and vulnerable in this first draft, knowing that successive ones will be better.

Read through your story several times. Does it have "fluff" in it? Fluff is details that aren't moving your story forward. Your story should have just the right number of elements. No more. No less. It also needs to be in its simplest form to be memorable and repeatable. The best brand stories are told in four or five short paragraphs that define the clients' challenges and your promise of transformation.

Summarize What You Learned

Your brand story should be the bridge between your purpose and your customers' struggles. Review your story. It should teach your clients more about you, your life, and your business purpose. It should reflect the struggles you know your clients are going through.

Is your purpose communicated well? Can someone glean your purpose from your story?

_____

_____

Does your story reflect your customer's journey and struggles?

_____

_____

chapter eight

The Intersection of Sales

Throughout our exercises, we've focused on the two perspectives that make up a solid brand: YOU and your clients. Both perspectives are equally as important, yet they can be misinterpreted as contrasting perspectives. To me, the magic of a brand is found at the intersection of those two perspectives, where your clients connect with your purpose. It manifests when your brand story and message inspire them to move forward to work with you. That intersection is a feeling, and that feeling happens when your clients come to understand that you can solve their problem and transform their lives.

Up to this point, you've identified your ideal clients, and you've discovered the talents and skills you bring to your business. You've written your letter to your tribe, identified the elements of your brand story, and put them together to tell your story in a powerful way.

The next piece of your branding puzzle is a deeper under-standing of the intersection of you and your client. The next lessons provide the final leg of your prospective customers' journey to that magical crossroads. You'll come to better un-derstand the buying process and factors that lead consum-ers to make purchases. You'll also tie everything you have learned so far into a digital sales process that highlights your expertise and the challenges your clients face in their journey to finding a solution.

CREATING THE EXPERIENCE

Why Clients Want to Work with You

How the world perceives your brand is everything. Your brand is multifaceted and is created through the experience you provide your clients. The experience is based on your deep understanding of who they are and what they need to be successful. Your brand is made up of three distinct things:

Number one: You—your expertise and experience, your personality and voice, your values and moral compass. Your expertise is the fuel behind your offerings and what makes them unique.

Number two: Your clients—the most important piece of your business. Without them, your business would not exist. How you connect to them is directly related to how well you understand them. You must understand what they feel, what they struggle with, and what they want. You must know how they speak of your services, what they are looking for, and the process they go through to decide when to engage your services.

Number three: Your business—the front face and brand of your business and what your clients feel about your business. This includes your logo, colors, your offerings, and how you promote them. It includes your storefront and brick-and-mortar shop, and the way you package your products. It encompasses all that your business represents to your clients and the public and the feelings your message and visuals invoke in them.

These three things combine to create the essence of your brand. You now understand that your brand is more than just a logo and colors. You've come to understand all the pieces that will make your business successful. Your brand is the human, public face of your business. It's the virtual storefront that welcomes people as they metaphorically choose to walk through your door. It's meant to inspire your clients and tell them they've found their solution. At its simplest level, your brand persuades clients to want to work with you and buy your services.

FOUR REASONS PEOPLE BUY YOUR SERVICES

People buy from people they know, like, and trust. They buy from people with whom they connect and have similar worldviews and experiences. They buy from people who make them feel valued. These are the reasons people make a purchase from you.

There is a science behind why people buy and from whom. Understanding the science will help you design a strategy for a brand message that convinces potential clients to choose you over your competitors. Competition is fierce. To stand out and above, you need to know and proclaim how you are different and better for your ideal clients.

Did you know there are four main reasons people buy from you? It's critical to include these four elements in your brand foundation to build a brand that connects with potential clients:

Number one: Clients buy from you because they connect to your purpose, your why—your brand story. It is the starting point for potential clients to get to know you and what drives you. It is one of the most important pieces to building a relationship with your clients.

Number two: Clients buy from you because you make them feel good about themselves and good about the world. Your ability to make your clients feel this is critical to making an impact on their world and their lives.

Number three: Clients buy from you because you provide more than just a transaction. Clients want more from you. They want to *feel* something. Giving them the feeling they crave will keep them coming back again and again. To build brand loyalty that drives referrals and repeat business, you must be willing to go that extra mile for your clients. You have to offer them more than just your end product. Think about how to offer transformation, hope, happiness, or other positive feelings. That is the mindset you need.

Number four: They buy from you because they trust you. Trust is a big part of any financial transaction. The customer needs to believe in you and your talents and have faith that you will fulfill your promise and deliver. Building trust is a huge piece of your brand.

The Four Reasons People Buy from You Exercise

What is your business purpose? What is the "why" behind your business? Refer back to the Define Your Purpose Exercise, in Chapter Six.

_____

_____

_____

_____

How do you show your purpose to the world?

_____

_____

_____

_____

How do you want your clients to feel after doing business with you?

_____

_____

_____

How can you elevate your offerings or delivery of them to make them more experiential? In other words, how can the delivery of your offerings be focused on the experience and not on the transaction?

_____

_____

_____

_____

Trust is a key piece of any sales transaction. List reasons your clients should trust you. Think credentials and experience.

_____

_____

_____

_____

How can you better communicate the reasons clients should trust you? Refer back to You're the Expert Exercise, in which you brainstormed your talents and expertise.

_____

_____

_____

_____

PUT IT INTO ACTION

Review your current messaging on your website, social media, signage, and hard copy, such as flyers and business cards. Identify areas in your messaging that could be more focused on why people buy from you.

_____

_____

_____

_____

CRAFTING YOUR BRAND JOURNEY

Your clients go through a decision-making process before purchasing. Along the way, they need information to support their decisions. If you want them to choose your business over your competitors, you must provide the information they need to make the decision to work with you. That information needs to be part of your messaging, your blog posts and videos, and what you communicate to your potential clients in other ways.

Understand that just because someone has a need doesn't mean that they are ready for the solution. It's your job to help clients identify that they need you, realize the struggle they are having, and inspire them to find a solution. That can only be done by your understanding of the journey they are going through.

Your clients are looking to solve problems, but their vision of success may not be your vision of success. I once had a client who was a dentist who had a patient with slightly crooked teeth. When she needed dental implants, he saw this as a perfect time to create a more beautiful smile for her. He painstakingly took the time to position each tooth perfectly. When he was finished, he revealed her perfect new teeth. To his dismay, she seemed disappointed.

What happened? He failed to ask her about *her* vision of perfect teeth. Her vision what not his vision. She identified her imperfect smile with her own image of perfection.

Don't do the same thing. Don't assume that your vision of a client's success is the same as his or her vision. Ask them what they want. Ask them what they are struggling with. Use questions that help you understand where they are faltering. Your insights into their struggles will lead you to a shared version of a successful outcome.

What would have made the dentist's job easier? Not only should he have asked about her expectations, but he should have also provided more information about the procedure. He should have encouraged discussion, provided information, and communicated the outcome.

Your clients need information along the way to make the right decision. Going back to the example of purchasing a car, my husband and I needed to know the available features, how those features provided a better driving experience, and the cost of those features before making a final decision. That kind of personalized information will empower your clients to envision their future and motivate them to purchase your solution to their problem or challenge.

CRAFTING THE JOURNEY EXERCISE

What information do your clients need during their research process? Think of questions you hear as they are working through making a decision. Think of the information they need as they are going from the beginning to the end of the decision process.

_____

_____

_____

_____

What do your clients need to know to make an informed decision? Think of the phrase, "You don't know what you don't know." Sometimes clients are not aware of the detailed information they should know to make a right decision.

_____

_____

_____

_____

What questions do clients often have when they are getting ready to work with you? Can you make a list and create an FAQ page on your website?

_____

_____

_____

_____

_____

_____

_____

Review the answers you've just brainstormed in the pro-
ceeding Crafting the Journey Exercise. Try to glean insight
into the best way to deliver the information your clients need
to make the decision to work with you.

What can you offer as a resource that provides information
your potential clients need in their decision-making process?
Consider webinars, onsite classes, blogs, or podcasts.

_____

_____

_____

_____

What transformation do your clients want to see within
themselves or their business?

_____

_____

_____

_____

What transformation do your clients need to make to be
successful?

_____

_____

_____

_____

SALES FUNNEL

A sales funnel is a path customers or clients follow in doing business with you. It positions information and offerings logically and channels clients seamlessly through an organized order. From the first thing clients buy to the next thing they need, there's an order to the way they need and seek products and services.

Through the exercises you have done so far, you have developed an understanding of the journey that your clients take before working with you. You know the questions they ask and the way they feel once they pass the tipping point and reach out to you. Your sales funnel should reflect this natural journey. It should include the information they need while researching and answers to their questions as they work through their decision-making process. There should be text, photo, and video approaches to engage them that recognizes and addresses their needs on a deep level. An effective sales funnel will convey that you are the expert they are looking for. This information should then lead them to purchase your offerings.

THE AIDA MODEL

AIDA is an acronym of the buying process: awareness, interest, desire, and action. The AIDA model highlights the four critical steps that people go through when making a decision to purchase.

Why is AIDA important? Savvy business owners create a connection with potential clients using their brands. This includes leveraging written content, videos, photography, message, and offerings in a way that fosters meaningful relationships throughout the buying process. Done right, your potential client will engage and want to work with you.

It starts with a deep understanding of your clients' journey and moves into how you can best support them as they advance through the steps.

A = Awareness

This first step is critical. People can't purchase from you if they don't know your business offerings exist as an option. They need to be aware of your business, what you offer, how you are different, and how your offerings help their problems.

I = Interest

Once someone becomes aware of your business, your next step is to spark their interest in learning more about you, what you do, who you are, and how you help them. To accomplish this, your website must be user-friendly, so potential clients can find information easily, learn more about you, and begin to engage. If a website is difficult to navigate or confusing, clients quickly lose interest. Your website should illustrate quickly and simply how you can help them make a change and solve their problem.

D = Desire

To create a customer's desire to make a purchase, your offers must hit the heart of your potential clients' issues or challenges. You must inspire or motivate them to change or show them they need your offerings in a foundational way. This includes words and images that identify your clients and demonstrate that you understand their problems. You must also show them how they will feel if their issues or challenges were resolved.

A = Action

The final step is the purchase. At this point, clients have realized that you are the expert they've been looking for, and they are ready to take action and purchase. This can include clicking to download a document or signing up for your workshop. For someone to have made it to this final step, they must have gone through the three preceding steps. The final step is the culmination of showing potential clients who you are, proving you understand their problem, and building trust and confidence that you will provide the solution they need.

The Sales Funnel Exercise

Offerings and Resources

Review the information you listed in the Crafting the Journey Exercise about what your clients need when making a decision. From that list, can you identify new resources that can attract potential clients?

_____

_____

_____

_____

To create a solid content strategy, you need to consider the way your potential clients want to consume the information they need to hear. That includes written content, blogs, podcasts, PDFs, video, webinars, social media campaigns, visual infographics, or any other formats that your clients may prefer to engage and learn. What are the most popular ways you feel your clients want to receive your resources?

_____

_____

_____

_____

What information can you provide that can build trust in your offerings? Think of tip sheets (Top 5 Tips, Top 5 Mistakes), case studies, portfolios, examples of your work, and testimonials. This is the information that you know your clients will need as they go through the decision-making process.

For each of your offerings, identify pieces of information or topics that would capture your clients' attention and create interest in your business. In other words, what do your clients need to understand to consider your offerings when starting their decision process?

_____

_____

_____

_____

For each of your offerings, identify the information your potential clients need that will build a desire for your offerings and lead to making the decision to purchase. In other words, what resources can you provide to answer the questions they ask as they make a final decision?

_____

_____

_____

_____

What pieces of information do your clients need before deciding to move forward? (Price, quality, how long it will take for you to provide the service.) This information needs to be easily accessible on your website so that they can make an informed decision.

_____

_____

_____

_____

Exercise and Examples of AIDA

HOW DO YOU STACK UP?

Awareness

The first step is making the right people aware that your business exists. Examples: free whitepaper, worksheet, webinar, social media marketing, contests, assessments, and free 30-minute consultation

What do you do to grow awareness of your business?

_____

_____

_____

_____

Interest

Now that your potential clients are aware of you and your offerings, how do you generate interest in working with you or purchasing your offerings? Examples: You demonstrate you understand their challenges and show an alternative to their struggles. You show why you're the expert and why they should trust in your solution. Other endeavors that foster interest include speaking, podcasting, and being a published author. These activities can simultaneously develop aware-ness and interest by building trust.

What are keywords you use to help clients know you understand them?

_____

_____

_____

_____

Do you prove your expertise and build trust through your message?

_____

_____

Do you identify the key benefits of working with you?

_____

_____

Desire

The next step is desire. This step takes potential clients' interest one step closer to purchasing from you. They need to have a clear vision that your offerings are the right solution for them and their current problems or challenges. That comes from your messaging and delivering consistent industry ex-pertise in all your marketing efforts.

For example, you demonstrate the benefits of resolving

their challenges, such as giving them more time to work on their business. You offer examples of how you have created processes and systems to scale business growth. You provide data that proves how you helped businesses attract more clients and be more competitive in their industry. Other examples are case studies showing measurable results and video testimonials showing the benefits of your offerings.

Review your sales pages and content. Can you identify areas that could be more concise?

Do you clearly communicate the end-benefits of working with you?

_____

_____

Do you encourage your clients to envision a world that is free of their current struggles?

_____

_____

Do you clearly identify your ideal clients with words that connect and relate to them?

_____

_____

Action

This step requires providing simple methods for making a purchase with minimal searching and clicking. Examples include a clear and easy-to-find buy button, next steps toward purchase button, contact information, and online calendar. Consider these questions:

Are the calls-to-action on each of your sales content pages clear? Do they lead to logical next steps?

_____

_____

_____

_____

Do clients see a clear way to contact you, work with you, or make a purchase?

_____

_____

Review how you market your events, workshops, classes, etc. Are the next steps toward purchase clearly stated within the description?

_____

_____

_____

_____

Does the purchase or sign-up process convey trust?

_____

_____

chapter nine

Your Brand Reimagined

As our business evolves, so does our brand. Since 2009 when my business was born, I have helped over 150 businesses rebrand themselves, and it wasn't until I had been in business for eight years that I recognized my business also needed a redesign. I felt there was a disconnect between the message on my website and how I was selling my services. The colors I had chosen no longer represented my audience or me. I reviewed my brand with a critical eye and realized it needed more.

Over time, my ideal clients had shifted. My early clients were startup businesses, a mix of men and women who had amazing ideas. That clientele evolved into focused, seasoned entrepreneurs, specifically more women-owned businesses. My clients had journeyed with me and reflected where I was now in my own business.

For my brand, that translated into deeper colors. The logo became more modern and sleek, adding an elegance to the brand that it hadn't had before. I then fully realized the power of the rebrand. I had completed these for so many clients, and I had the opportunity to experience it myself.

I went to my graphic artist and gave her the task. I told her I wanted my business to "grow up." With that one request, I was able to refine my message and realize a new look that better connected with my ideal clients. The visual logo and colors took on more depth through pure, deeper tones. The messaging changed to express that I work with purpose-driven entrepreneurs and speak directly to them and their struggles.

With every rebrand, it comes down to three key elements: you, your clients, and your business.

You, Your Clients, and Your Business Exercise

Your business evolves—and so should your brand. This exercise will help you assess how well your current brand reflects your current business.

You

You are your brand. If your mindset shifts in significant ways, your brand needs to reflect that shift. If you've made huge strides in your industry and expertise but are still using the same brand, you are not showcasing all that you have become.

Has your mindset changed dramatically in how you view yourself, your business, or the world? How is your mindset different now than it was before at the start of the "old" brand?

_____

_____

_____

_____

Do you see a different vision or purpose for yourself from what you had before? If so, what is that vision and purpose, and how has it changed?

_____

_____

_____

_____

Is your expertise fully communicated in your offerings and solutions?

_____

_____

Your Clients

Your clients are the foundation of your brand. If you find they are shifting to a new demographic, or new mindset, then your brand must shift with them. From your offerings to your visual brand, you must incorporate your clients' ideals and values into your brand foundation.

When you look at your clientele, do you see a shift in who you are serving? If so, is it a demographic, geographic, or mindset shift?

_____

_____

Do you find that there's a shift in what you are selling? Are you proportionately selling more of something now than you did in the past? Maybe you've added new offerings that are no longer being fully represented.

_____

_____

If you see a shift, what has happened to your client base to trigger that shift? For example, your clients are no longer the same, or they have matured or changed in a way to shift your offering balance. Identify and list how your clients have changed.

_____

_____

Your Business

The words and images you use to represent your business are essential. From your offerings to your visual brand, you must connect with your ideal clients. All aspects of your marketing and promotions are based on who they are and how to reach them. If they change, your business strategy must change to continue to connect with them.

You may need to realign your brand with where your business is heading and its new vision, purpose, and mission. This includes updating your marketing with a new visual brand, offerings, and promotions for your new audience.

This exercise will help you understand if it is time to update your brand and marketing.

Has your business shifted its long-term goal?

_____

_____

_____

Do you see a new vision or end-goal for your business?

_____

_____

_____

Has your business purpose shifted?

_____

_____

_____

Do you see a major shift in the foundation of why your business exists? For example, if you now want to exit the market rather than grow the business.

_____

_____

_____

THE JOURNEY TO SUCCESSFUL MARKETING

Achieving marketing success is a learning process. It's a journey. To be successful, you need to continually reassess what you are doing right and what is no longer working. You also need to review the needs of your clients to ensure you are offering them the right information they need to be successful. This chapter is designed to help you evaluate your current visual brand and to create a strategy for ongoing success.

YOUR VISUAL BRAND

Your brand is so much more than just logo, colors, and fonts. Every visual piece of your brand needs to communicate the vision you have for your business. It must also convey the transformation you promise your clients and the feeling you want to promote to the world. That's a tall order, but it can be done effectively with the proper intention and guidance.

The imagery that is the visual face of your brand needs to inspire the same values and culture that you've created for your business through your journey. The pictures you choose for your website must elevate your business above the competition. They must also align with your purpose and connect with your ideal clients. A lot is riding on good visuals to communicate your brand message. No pressure here.

A good visual brand extends and tells your story beyond words. Visuals are as significant as words—maybe more so. The wording used in branding provides only a fraction of the message perceived. A picture is worth a thousand words, and images offer abstract and emotional information that words can't provide. To be most effective, images must be in sync with the wording and be consistent with or complementary to the color tones of your brand. They should blend into the overall message, supporting the written content and not standing out of place.

A visual brand humanizes all the aspects of your business. It reminds people they are doing business with other people. It's important to include photography that reflects the people in your business, whether the front face of your business is you alone or a team of people working alongside you. Remember that your business is more than just a name. Your brand must build that human connection from the computer or smartphone to the hearts of your ideal clients. If you are your brand, then your image needs to be a big part of the visual brand.

COLOR THEORY

We may not be consciously aware of it, but the colors that surround us have a profound effect on our emotional well-being. The colors we choose to represent our business make an emotional statement to our customers. Choosing the right colors is a significant piece of building a solid brand that aligns with your values and culture.

What do colors mean to most people? Colors have both positive and negative connotations; so make sure you choose your colors well. Listed below are some common associations of color and emotion. These associations can vary between individuals and can be seen as positive or negative, depending upon your use of that color and its association. Your colors should be interpreted positive by you and your target audience.

Red
- Positive: high energy, power, passion, strength, demands attention
- Negative: stop, anger, danger

Orange
- Positive: courage, confidence, enthusiasm, optimistic, friendly
- Could be perceived as negative or positive, depending on the client: autumn, Halloween

Yellow
- Positive: creativity, bright, energy, uplifting, assists in mental clarity
- Negative: associated with illness and quarantine, warning, hard to read on a computer screen

Green
- Positive: healing, health, nature, balance, growth, money, freshness
- Negative: inexperience, envy, misfortune

Turquoise
- Positive: spiritual, self-expression, energizing, protection, intuition, creative
- Could be perceived as negative or positive,

depending on the client: feminine

Blue
· Positive: honesty, trust, dependability, security, intelligence, calm, peaceful
· Negative: can represent sadness and depression, cold, technology

Purple
· Positive: wealth, power, royalty, nobility, ambition
· Could be perceived as negative or positive, depending on the client: feminine

Gold
· Positive: established, wealth, prosperity, valuable, wisdom, generosity, high quality
· Negative: gaudy, ostentatious

Silver
· Positive: elegant, graceful, sleek, sophisticated, uplifting
· Negative: grief
· Could be perceived as negative or positive, depending on the client: maturity and old age

White
· Positive: clean, fresh, pure, innocence, goodness
· Negative: can come across as stark or sterile

Black
· Positive: formal, dramatic, classy, authority, power, sophistication
· Negative: symbolizes death, evil, mystery

TYPOGRAPHY

Typography is the creative use of fonts, an essential element to a strong business brand. Fonts can elicit many feelings and give a sense of modern or classic by the slant or weight of the font. It's no wonder fonts play a critical role in the overall perception of a brand.

It's important when choosing fonts to know your demographics and target audience. You want your typography to match their perception of your business and to reflect where your business is heading. There are hundreds of fonts to choose from, so you will want to hire a talented graphic artist to create a logo using a font that best represents you and your business.

Fonts that are offered free, or public use web-based fonts, may not be the best choice for your business website. A good graphic designer has access to many paid professional quality fonts that can provide just the right impact for your messaging. Unique fonts, appropriately paired, can be as impactful as the message. Whether on your desktop or for your website, ensure you install a font with the proper font licensing.

Here are a few examples of different fonts, some are free, and others are paid licensed fonts. You can see that the fonts chosen here are distinctly different and certainly show a different attitude in each example.

Hillda: Believe in yourself. Value your talents, gifts, and knowledge. Be willing to do the hard work.

Lora: Believe in yourself. Value your talents, gifts, and knowledge. Be willing to do the hard work.

Allura: Believe in yourself. Value your talents, gifts, and knowledge. Be willing to do the hard work.

Roboto: Believe in yourself. Value your talents, gifts, and knowledge. Be willing to do the hard work.

Violeta: Believe in yourself. Value your talents, gifts, and knowledge. Be willing to do the hard work.

Crete Round: Believe in yourself. Value your talents, gifts, and knowledge. Be willing to do the hard work.

YOUR LOGO

Logos are deceptively simple. They play a significant role in how we perceive brands and convey many things in a small space. They must be memorable, distinctive, and unique. The design process for creating a new logo considers you and your business and how you want clients to perceive your brand. It also considers your target audience and your industry. You want to ensure your logo will be relevant for years.

A strong logo:

- · Is simple.

- · Represents your business and you.

- · Looks good and is legible in small spaces (like your website or a business card).

- · Is versatile and functional.

- Clearly communicates your business name.
- Should look good in a variety of formats and on various media.

STRIKING PHOTOGRAPHY

I know you've asked yourself this: Do I really need custom photography for my website? I'll answer that with another question: Do you want your business to stand out as professional and unique?

Visual pictures communicate quicker than words. The images you choose on your website need to be as unique as you and your business. They should also be in alignment with your values and culture. Nothing screams amateur louder than smartphone snapshots and random stock photos that are thrown up on a website without thought or cohesiveness.

If you want to boost your business up a notch and be taken seriously as an expert, you must have a strategy to create a cohesive visual message on your site. That almost always includes custom photography.

Color Theory Exercise

Color Theory as Applied to Your Brand

List eight of your business values as from Your Business Culture Exercise from chapter six. These are the values that are important to you and your clients and are the foundation of your business culture. Then, next to your values, list the colors that best reflect and represent each value. Do the colors your values represent match your brand colors?

Brand Value	Colors
Honesty	Blue

TYPOGRAPHY BASICS AS APPLIED TO YOUR BRAND

Identify the fonts used on your website. Are they in alignment with the foundation of your brand? In other words, if your brand is forward thinking in an industry constantly changing (like web design) are your brand fonts reflective of those trends? In my case, yes, the fonts I am using for my brand are modern, light, and unique—just as Blue Zenith stands within the industry.

VISUAL BRAND REVIEW AND EXERCISE

Review your current visual brand, including the fonts, colors, logo, and pictures. Can you pinpoint what is not authentic to you?

_____

_____

_____

_____

Can you brainstorm images that better reflect your purpose? Your business culture?

_____

_____

_____

_____

Can you imagine images that convey your future vision of your business?

_____

_____

_____

_____

EXERCISE TO IDENTIFY YOUR VISUAL BRAND

- Create a Pinterest mood board that showcases pictures that visually match the heart of you and your business personality.

- Create a Pinterest mood board that showcases pictures that reflect what you want your business to be known for. Think about visually capturing that feeling or essence of what you want your clients to feel after working with you.

- Create a Pinterest mood board that showcases the culture and values of your business.

chapter ten

Go Ahead. Dream Big.

Congratulations! You've worked through all the exercises and have gained insights into yourself and your clients that you didn't have before. You have used these insights to create an actionable plan to communicate your brand values, story, and messaging with increased intention and clarity. That brings us to the last piece of the branding puzzle—stepping fully into your possibilities, believing in yourself, and committing to putting your authentic self into your brand message.

You are the final piece to making this happen, and that can be intimidating. Your ability to succeed in creating the vision you have for yourself, your life, and your business boils down to courage. You must be brave enough to take the first step. Then you must continuously push yourself outside your comfort zone and into the realm of your brilliance. That only happens when you've stepped through your fear, into the unknown, into the place that equally scares and excites you.

To support you as you move forward in your branding journey, I've created the acronym BRAVE. I see BRAVE as packed with meaning. I challenge you to be brave in every sense of the word and embrace all that is you.

B = Be bold in who you are. Don't hide your brilliance. Don't compromise what makes you thrive and do your best.

R = Be real in taking the journey. You can't change your past or the way people around you think or act, but you can take responsibility. You can choose the way you want to react to the forces you see as friction and continually move forward. Be real about your journey, accept who you are, and use your story to fuel the impact you'll make on this world.

A = Be authentic. Be yourself and true to your heart. Tell your story as only you can tell it, with confidence and boldness. There are no comparisons to your journey. It's yours and yours alone. Accept the lessons you learned and the impact they made on your life and journey.

V = Be vulnerable. To be authentic, you need to connect with the vulnerable part of your story. Don't be afraid to share your weaknesses and challenges. They are what make you stronger. Sharing your vulnerability also helps clients relate to you as a real person.

E = Be empowered. You are perfect just the way you are. Believe in your purpose and the impact you want to make in this world. Believe in yourself and your value, including your expertise and unique insights. You are the foundation of your brand. Empower your brand with the power of you!

ALIGN YOUR BRAND WITH YOUR PURPOSE

Your brand encompasses so much more than what you had probably imagined when you first opened this workbook. I hope you've learned more about yourself, your business, and how to tell your story so you can connect with your ideal clients and impact their lives and businesses. I hope you've thought through the experience you provide and how you want your clients to feel. Remember, the heart of your brand is the feeling your clients have after doing business with you.

It is within your grasp to craft your business to reach your vision of success—the vision you wrote about in one of the very first exercises in this workbook. If you believe you are the master of your destiny, you can create the life and business you envision. Belief in yourself and determination will make it happen. You must know in your heart that your light shines brilliantly. Your gifts are unique, and you have the power to make a difference in the lives of those you work with. That power comes from confidence and belief that you can change the world.

I CHALLENGE YOU TO DREAM BIG

In the beginning of this book, I spoke about the three non-negotiables of success and how hard it is to stay true to them. They are:

- · Believe in yourself.
- · Value your talents and gifts and knowledge.

· Be willing to do the hard work.

These three non-negotiables of success are the core of your superpower and separate you from everyone else. When you believe in your superpower, you can help improve your clients' lives and businesses. Just because you are a small business does not mean you make a small impact. You will make a difference that no one else can.

By now, your journey has helped you understand your superpowers—how you are unique and how you are meant to impact your clients. You have also gained insight into your ideal clients and a better understanding of their journey and challenges. Leverage your newfound insights—your client letter, your story, your offerings, benefits, and value—into your message.

I encourage you to take what you have learned from this book and bring it to life in your business and your digital marketing. Your message needs to shout to the world that you are the one distinct solution for your struggling clients. The world is a better place because of you and your talents. By embracing your purpose, you take control of the impact you make and will create a brand that that ensures the world knows it.

acknowledgments

This book is a culmination of my own journey. Ten years operating a small business means dedication and commitment. This book would not have happened without the support of so many extraordinary people in my life. For them and their help I am thankful.

To my husband, Andy, I am grateful for your ever-present love and support. Without that, this journey and this book would have been nearly impossible. You pick up the slack in so many ways and keep life as normal as possible while living with an entrepreneur. Not a small feat!

To my son, Alex, your adventurous, independent, and gentle spirit inspires me. When you came to work at Blue Zenith after college, it had been me—and me alone—running the business. Together, we have built this business to where it is. Without your time and energy, patience, and willingness, I would not have had the time to dedicate to writing this book. You have walked beside me each day, building this dream to change the world one entrepreneur at a time.

To my daughter, Andrea, you have taught me the true meaning of living a purposeful life. I'm inspired by the way you design your life from dream to reality. Your adventures have shown me that it's possible to achieve just about anything—as long as you believe in yourself and your ability to make it happen. That same spirit is foundational in this book. You exemplify exactly what I am striving for in my life, each day—that unwavering belief in myself to walk boldly towards a purposeful life.

To my mother, your belief in me has given me the wings to fly. This book is proof of that.

To my mentor and friend, Kimberly Alexander, you have been instrumental in my seeing my own path and possibilities. Your guidance, support, and belief in me are the reason this book was even possible. You allowed me to see big things for myself.

To my friend and confidante, Katie Myers, you are one of bravest people I know. Your fearless courage and common-sense values will take you far in life and in business. It is that sense of self that inspires me to be better each day. You have taught me more about standing bravely and boldly in the face of challenges than anyone else—and that is the entrepreneurial spirit that I encourage through the stories in this book.

To my accountability partner and friend, Jacki Cox, you helped me focus on the next task at hand. That may sound simple, but the mind is sometimes hard to quiet. Thank you for reigniting my creativity and holding me accountable when I needed it the most.

To my clients and fellow entrepreneurs, you inspire me with your grit and perseverance. I have seen your struggles and because of you, have been inspired to write this book. The world needs each of you to be bold and brave. I know your challenges, and I strive to do better each day to honor your hard work.

To the entire My Word Publishing team, I thank you for

your guidance through this process. A huge special thank you goes out to my editor, Catherine Spader, who made this a fun project and brought out the best in my writing.

about the author

After more than fifteen years as a software engineer in the corporate world, Donna Galassi founded her business, Blue Zenith, a digital branding and web design firm. As an expert digital brand strategist, web designer, consultant, author and speaker, Donna enjoys working with entrepreneurs, and has been blessed to have given wings to hundreds of clients, helping others to find their voice amongst many in small business. With clients across the nation, Donna has been instrumental in building brands that have launched businesses into success. Donna is the founder of the "Go Ahead. Dream Big." programs, educating entrepreneurs through her professional philosophy of reimagining branding, and providing practical strategies to entrepreneurs and small businesses. To invite Donna to speak at your next event, or to learn more about how you can build your brand and grow your empire, visit BlueZenith.com.

When Donna isn't working on building brands, she enjoys travelling the world with her husband, Andy and two young adult children. Her philosophy is that life is an adventure, and is lived through enjoying hiking, biking and snowboarding in Colorado's beautiful Rocky Mountains.